LOVE MOMENTS

LOVE MOMENTS

Kendall Wilhide

Cover design by Neuwirth & Associates
Interior Design by Neuwirth & Associates

Vantage Press and the Vantage Press colophon
are registered trademarks of Vantage Press, Inc.
FIRST EDITION
All rights reserved, including the right of
reproduction in whole or in part in any form.

Copyright © 2011 by Kendall Wilhide
Published by Vantage Press, Inc.
419 Park Ave. South, New York, NY 10016
Manufactured in the United States of America

ISBN: 978-1-533-16434-9

Library of Congress Catalog Card No.: 2010917367

0 1 2 3 4 5 6 7 8 9

To Havilah.

Contents

Dreams of Life	1
My Teacher, Teach Me	3
A Place Called Home	5
My Family Tree (Part I)	7
Our Family Tree (Part II)	9
Comfortable Dry	12
In the Grasp of Life Unfolding	14
The Unnoticed	16
Through the Eyes of the Guilty	18
A Place Forgotten	20
As the Trumpets Call	22
Ripples in the Water	24
In the Cool Desert Rain	26
On the Water's Edge	28
Night Has Fallen	30
The End of a Dark Day	32
Through My Open Door	35
As We Enter the Rose of His Feast	37
In the Auburn Cradle of the Night	39
The Sound of the Sea	41
The Rain of That Day	43
Creation Set Free	45
In the Glance of a Hurricane	47
In a Ray of Hope	49

Love Restored	51
Captured in Your Green Array	53
Unbeknownst and Unseen Woman of My Dreams	54
To My Fairy Queen	56
She Has the Prettiest Face	58
A Place Where Our Eyes Collide	59
In One Love of One Song	61
Where My Lover Waits	63
The Lights Behind the Scene	65
Time	67
A Moment Tender Caught in Time (Part I)	68
A Moment Tender Captured in Dream (Part II)	69
My Vision of Vienna	71
In the Heart of Vienna	72
The Glow of the Magic Beans	74
Tiramisu	76
My Little Lass	77
A Knock at the Door	79
Sacred, Secret, Sweetie	81
One, Hot, Kiss	83
Climax!	85
Hot!	87
The Burning Thread of Your Whisper	89
My Taste of Delight	91
My Little Liquid Electric Love	92
Salt	94
When Ships Collide	95
Two Unlikely Champions	97
Check Point Charlie	99
A Trip to Starbucks	101
The Platinum Girl from NYC	103

My Lovely Little Villain	105
My Little Gypsy Queen	106
A Place Within	108
The Other Side of the Mirror	110
My Spiritual Dream	111
As to Her Dreams I Sway	113
My Heart	115
Where My Lover Waits	116
A Place Where Our Eyes Collide	118
In the Eyes of a Stranger	120
In This Dream That's Real	122
The Knights of the Light	124
Wherever You Stand	126
I've Seen the Spirit Cry	127
When All Seemed Lost	130
Walking in Heaven	132
God's Word to You	134
Where the Sun Split the Heavens	136

LOVE MOMENTS

Dreams of Life

We are two of a kind that are one
In the spirit of the Lord
You are the song that fills my heart.

As the words in me abound
That falls into my deepest well
Touched by you invisibly, soft spoken without a sound.
A paper cut that bleeds me dry

The welling in my eye
The pain within my stomach's pit
The reason I am alive

To strive with you unto a better voice
Of what the world should be
Of love, not hate, in the victory conquered in faith
Not fait

To see the dawning of resolve
Within our hearts set free.
As I hold your hand and walk with thee
Past that line to see all creation overflow
In life's divine reprieve.

My Teacher, Teach Me

A Teacher of minds
A Teacher of souls in the Lord
In the fire in which inside her, she holds
Completely given

As before her, it unfolds
A promise given unto heart on high
Kept to its finish from the very start
Of what is truly a treasure
Of the unseen, of what's foretold

In the quiet of a moment
In a single second, a division bold
She took a step into the arms of the new
From the embrace of the cold hands of the old

Into the face of what she feared
Released as a thunderstorm into the one
To whom she is endeared

As the things of this world fall away from her clay
This burning flame, relinquished into the rising sun
She looks to me and she sees we are both the same.

A Place Called Home

A man not of means,
All he has is a wooden room
With a window, and a good view
A big brass bed
With comforters, all worn and faded
Homey, warm and cozy

As the fire crackles in an amber glow
The ambers spark and pop
As he sits down beside her
His arms placed around her
Held gently in place

As he brushes his fingers down her face
To feel the softness and the sweetness of her taste
To feel her release and melt into his embrace
No words spoken,
No exhilaration made in haste

Just the calm of the smoldering fire's gentle burning
Into a night blessed
All that hinders its merging, now unleashed

This place that is my hold, my heart
To open wide a place that is warm inside
A place I want you to call your home

My Family Tree

(Part I)

We drink the living water
One our family tree
As we tone all the colors of the rainbow alive
All the branches sound in harmony
All the leaves sing, set free
To the voice of a falling sky.

Each drop bled from the heart of Heaven
Each drop a crystal city
Each drop, the dew from God's Garden
Set loose from the grasp of futility.

We lay on hands, a touch of life
To heal each other's hearts
From the tire treads left behind
From the lips of a lie left in the cold of a poison rain
From a hand enraged into a fist
And from the holes of the fiery darts.

In a place we've never been before
Where we stand as one
As we come into it in each other
We feel the warmth of the Son
Our wounds they heal
Our scars disappear
Where tears of joy are now revealed.

To hold and be held
In a love so true, so powerful, so awesome
That makes me feel anew.

That harkens to the distant cry in the words "it is done,"
As now true life has begun.

Our Family Tree

(Part II)

Of everyone of this family tree
Each has a defining grace
A gift given from up on high
As His light shines upon our face.

Of many colors, and many shades
Vivid, burning bright
All unique, well defined
Yet one in the Father's sight.

That in our hearts reveals His Son
That emerges from within
That ruptures out from every pore
That burns upon our skin.

We fit together, each piece of a puzzle
That illuminates in traits
Reigning together of Heaven on earth
As its fire culminates

Each joint binds one to another
To all our different parts
Predestined to come, unto His calling
United in all our fates.

That become one crystal, with many sides
As many rainbows collide
A promise kept, of tears we've wept
Of what we've left behind.

We closed the doors on the past
As we find another waiting
Left wide open to embrace

As we peel away the cast and from what suffocates
No longer found, as the girdle of restraint
Now becomes unlaced and the onion peels fall to the ground

We, the Daughters and Sons of Liberty
The branches of this living tree
A hedge of wild roses growing together
In the Father's garden
In overflow we stand, our spirits as one set free
Of spirit walking on the earth
Of His light in a very darkened world
Of the Christ that harkens in our hearts
Of His brilliance that set before us unfurls.

When two or three or more come together
Of this family tree
The light's glow begins to grow
Until it is all that you can see

As we come into view
My little tiramisu to bear witness unto His face
As all the stars, in the night sky
Fall out of their place.

The morning star rising in us all
As by the new the old is now replaced
And the scars, and the stains of our prior nature
Now stand erased.

Comfortable Dry

The window's open, the sand's on fire,
On a lonely highway the tires
Of my convertible ragtop Riviera
Sound like a quire.

The dirt devils twirl
As over my head they touchdown.
The desert bakes from the sun
That burns away the shade
As it's rays rain down.

I light a cigarette
That dries my mouth
As I sip a pint of bourbon.
As this quenching, I douse,
The sand moves like a dancer in the rippling wind.
As it blows the arid air, I wipe the sweat
From my chin.

Traveling hot, the engine roars
A cool ninety, the needle soars.
Leaving vapors far behind.
I hear words whispered as lonely spirits whine.
There are no maps for were I'm going
There are no questions only knowing.
The road is lonely, covered in white
As the sun sets into the night.

In the Grasp of Life Unfolding

In the deluge of winter's heart, I walk with you alone
The only song, the gust of a snowy drone
Swirling and dancing to the wings of a fairy unseen

Only known in dream
We kick up heels and dance; two kids in laughter
Hearing the voice of romance
As the harp of an angel plays to our accord
Of two sprites in rhythm of a heart restored

Breathing your breath, seen in the air set free
From the exuberance left rosy upon your face, panting
Your eyes like stars, your face melting
Shimmering from the light,
The snow and ice dripping from your chin

Catching our breath we shine from within
An avalanche that roars down the mountain side

The cascade of a thousand rainbows, set free
In the pull of Nature's grip

Your fingers around my head tightly
As you gaze into my eyes
You look severely into my soul
As you kiss me in surprise

I brush my fingers across her cheek
So soft and alive
To see a single tear in joy
Streak from her eye
That fell into the broken place,
Held deep within my heart
That became a sea of liquid gold
That blew my doubts apart

To find a pot of soothing love
A treasure worth far more than gold
To fill my day with her warmth
That melts away the cold

The Unnoticed

Caught between two worlds,
The door left swinging.
The shadowed faces without any feeling
Left out in the cold.

In a blinding rain,
I walk in the dark of a cloudy day
Not knowing where my feet are going
Not hungry,
But inside empty
Of what this pale world to me in showing.

I pass the strangers in the street
All alone.
I stand in the crowds waiting for the train
Every eye unknown.
No words to speak, all voices numb and bleak.

Brushing up next to the girl next to me

Seeming so distant.
All touches that breech my space
Feel like the air so meek.

I dwell in a bustling ghost town
Pale dreams go silent by,
Not even aware of a pounding heart in me
That has barely survived.

All gray and white, no sun
No light
Just city lights
That are my only friend,
The only color my eyes recognize.
Their rays, the only light that's warms.
Their unnoticed stance,
Their unheard advance,
Their embrace,
The only thing in this haze
Without any scorn.

Through the Eyes of the Guilty

Clink, Clink,
The echoing of the empty cartridges
Singing and dancing as they bounce off the cold concrete floor.
In the chill of the lightless room
As in the dark of the night
The blood pours.

From a faceless name,
To whom life's no more than game,
That's played like chess
Except a little more time.

No opponent, just a silent footstep,
The only sound a silencer as it is being
Wound into place.
Before the last thing you see
Is a pillow coving your face.

A quiet peace is disturbed
As your cat leaves the room.
The only witness to your final quickness
Are pigeons on the ledge
Before your remains are exhumed,
From the restlessness of the blood curdled tomb.

Sunglasses cover the eyes
Of a ghost that lives in disguise,
Carrying a bag of tens and twenties
As onto the "friendly skies,"
This living executioner flies.

A Place Forgotten

In another time, in a place forgotten
Where the clocks move very slow
In a forest primeval through the deepest trees
Where you can feel the shadows glow

Beneath your feet where resides discreet,
The ancient beating heart of a land unknown
Except for a precious few

As even too few, this place is shown
Within the shadows mist, she sits
Beneath the throbbing moon
Silver rays touch her face to the sound of the month of June

A walking mystery shrouded in dreams
In a cloak that bewilders

A temptress, my enchanted one
With crystal green eyes
That hide behind the invisible clouds;
her secret that cannot be denied

The words written unseen between the lines
Hide, spoke only in our dreams
That if were said would be forbidden
But surely carried on a stream

As The Trumpets Call

Captured by the magic of an autumn spell
In the arms of a lover as we begin to swell
The sweat it pours off, that beads like pearls
To know she holds me in a night extreme

To feel my green-eyed queen come into the fabric of my being
Like a finger-tight dream
To feel the pulse of life perspire in boiled blood
And the swelter of a hot steamy summer's hoedown

Exploding into a storm of the call of the night owl
A jamboree set free in us
As from the sky split open raining fire
We take shelter and make the thunder
And the lightening plunder.

Of the calling of world coming together
In sounds of a mighty crash,

From within the sheet of many layers
Of silk from down under.

Ripples in the Water

In a pool of water, calm and dead
You are the pebble thrown in
That ripples eternally
An ebbing current that never stops
That flows through me in a place where no one can see

The force interjected, injected in me
That saves me from life's lonely shelf
Reprieved a song in silence
Heard in the distance of a the cold, black night
A light not yet seen, received

To come upon me like the beginning day
That embraces the morning
That encompasses the day
That can take the hand of one from the past
Into the arms of what can last

In the view of two lives as one
Of colors that collide before the rising sun
Profusion of life comes alive
Beyond its brim to overflow.

In the Cool Desert Rain

Staring from behind bleary eyes,
I feel a set of hands, fingers gently touch my face
Softer than velvet, warmer than lace

That cradles my head
As I look up to see your face
Held in the hold of your gaze
A beautiful longing forlorn
Piercing deep into me touched just right

Being touched like no other
Feeling everything inside oscillate, gyrate, orate,
Time stands still in the grace of an angel's embrace.

As the light of your lips I taste
Like the scent of honeysuckle
Its sweetness emulates through my mouth

Into the canyons of my heart,
No longer left in the dark of my lonely haggard soul.

Reborn, renewed, made alive once more
Like the desert in a spring rain
As it blossoms beneath an April rainbow
The threatening sky, grey blue
Bulges to the earth bursting open
This desert storm through eyes so green, so blue

Imparted unto me from you
One tear that's yours
Falls into my skies
As I feel fear pass away
I begin to heal

In the wake of the song
That spills of two as one
Together in its love we bathe
That removes the stain of a thought that's cruel
Now fallen away as one we melt into the rays of the sun.

On the Water's Edge

She pulls my tab like an old can of beer
As the thunder inside of me begins to peal
The claps get louder
As her form approaches sharp and sheer

Her hands draw near
The magic behind her playful eyes reveal a mystery
That leers into my beating drum
A ship lost at sea.

Upon the water's deepest waves
That plays into her hands
That holds me in her desire's whim
As over me the shadow stands

At her command
Her smiling face tones in treachery's desire
As she grabs me from behind
Unable to escape her grip of steel

Alluring are her hands
Her fingertips burning
Her teeth on my earlobe churning
As I melt into her grasp
All my inhibitions fade away.
As I surrender to her at last.

Night Has Fallen

Night has fallen once again
Upon a day of gray
Outlined only by the trees
Everyone else so far away

Except for you, my comrade in arms
My sister, my love so true
My warrior princess with a pure heart
My ally my friend, my Joan of Arc drenched in blue

We share a foxhole in the rain
Of a thousand bullets fired from eyes unknown
Our hands on our rifles
Helmets on our head
Our other hands together sown

In a grip so tight, in a trust entwined in might
In a glance of a thousand words unspoken

Captured in a web of the human heart
Both torn and both broken

I have her back, she has mine
Steeped in a desire that is divine
A map imprinted upon our souls
Since the beginning that in our oneness is defined

Drowning in blood, as we hear weary the battle field groan
Tired of the war, man must fight
To get to the final door
To see the dawning of a brand new day
To bear witness to all of creation restored

To stand in the pouring of Heaven's rain
A sight that cannot be ignored
To have the stain of war washed away
To have the taste of life reborn in us to stay.

The End of a Dark Day

I light up a cigarette and look across the darkened roads
Only the street lights glow
I feel you across the distance of the sea of time and space
Calling out my name

Unknown to a world outside
Unknown to the human eye
I hear you breathe in my heart
I feel your hands take hold

That holds me close in your grip
And will not let me go.
Alone together, you hold me near

Through eyes of tears with no fear
Broken as me, your soul it bleeds
Through your eyes that shed a tear

The blood of the soul spills to the ground
I cannot find a voice
That screams in silence enraged in truth
Unspoken without a choice.

You try to hide the pain away
Behind a smiles lie that cannot stop
The way you feel
A truth you cannot deny

That cuts right through the hungry heart
That rips the stone apart
No place to hide from what in you has died
An ache inside that cries for a new start
That long to see the sun rise over the sea of a new day.

Crashing upon a shore of hope
Of no denial, of being reborn
In a world that won't betray
That will not leave you to die alone.

That in love won't leave
But will stay
That will embrace not judge
That will not push you away.

I sit in silence in a world that is asleep

And dream of your broken eyes
So lost and so deep

To feel your hand upon me rest
To see the emptiness filled
In comfort soothed within my arms
And the unrest within you stilled.

Through My Open Door

In a place thought-forgotten
Left all alone
In a room with a candle
In the dark with just a dusty phone.

A door wide open
A window stares outside onto a road left untouched
As all around the reflection flickers
Of memories scattered on the floor, prone

Upon this room that nobody knows
The sun never rises
The night prolonged
It does not end

That longs for even surprises
That listens for a distant whisper
A call that never comes

The sound, only silence in abundance
So loud it sounds like drums
When all seemed lost
And all hope gone
But wait, a light comes on

She walked through my jagged door
Her hips swayed and her brilliance sounded
As shadows upon her face
Forlorn fell gently to the floor

Her heart opened wide and shed a tear
Revealing a smile behind the storm
The sunlight rose for the very first time
That splintered through my window
As our fingers touched in one accord.

The heart burned through this frozen room
And melted the ice away
Of this lonely room
My heart thought gone away.

Found again, forgotten no more
As home to me came through my open door.

As We Enter the Rose of His Feast

Captured in the nostalgic ways
Of something of the past
Not left behind, but not quite the same

As she drifts into another day
As much as she still holds
And she still reminisces through a shoe box
Of yesterday

It does not hold a candle
Of the things she now has to say
That more than a dream
For more than what's seemed
More than what meets the eye
Of what she holds dear

As now it comes here
Within our very grasp

To see upon a golden sea
A golden vessel's reprieve

A ship that sails with rainbow sails
To a place in your face
That requires faith to exist
That calls to the heart of a dreamer
That lovingly will no longer wait

Relinquishes fate to take hold of destiny
Who will not hesitate
In all her wrath to clear the slate

Of something more than what's behind the door
Of a thousand crying eyes
To have in them a change of heart
As it opens in surprise

I stand with you my shining star
In the door's frame
Held within one fire
Our embrace in one release

Beyond the taste of desire
Into a world we both let go
And feel eternal peace
Of the touch of God's hand
As we enter the rose of his feast.

In the Auburn Cradle of the Night

Let's turn down the lantern really low
And move to something slow
In this cabin made of earth and wood
Let's sway to the candle's glow

The wind outside gusts and blows
The feeling ominous to the sound that crows
That shrills like a freight train as it goes by
In a hundred miles of hungry sky

But you and I, we hold on
In the auburn crackle through the night
So warm, so tight
The shining of our touch, amber bright

My arms enthralled around my lover
Honed and taught
Enfold, engraved into one's skin
Where one ends and where one begins

Sown into one garment
In our beings
Dancing, two silhouettes, twins advancing
Until just one shadow remains

A glove adorned, tighter than skin
Deeper than what meets the eye
Closer than the warmest hug
Far more inside than anyone ever thought there could be

In a spark
A key that opened the door
That our spirits free adjoined into one
As we melt into what is unseen

Of what is beyond this human coil
Beyond man's wildest dreams
Into a place, not known before
Into a place now seen

The Sound of the Sea

I love the roar of the ocean
I love the smell of the sea
The way it makes me feel inside
Its breath that brings life to me

Kind of like you my sweetheart
You are a walking sea
An ocean of wonder of golden light
In your touch that has set me free

And like the ocean's rage
And its calm
You can be the same
A billowing sky, ominous about to unleash its wrath

Or a gentle blue from which your peace ensues
Wrapped in a blanketed wind, covering me
In your cloak of whispers

In the night, drenched in the water of your love
So warm, and held so tight

The Rain of that Day

As the spirit falls upon us,
Fall into me
I will fall into you
And we will hold each other up
During the heaviness of this heavenly rain.

When you feel you are going to crumble
Stand within my heart
And make it your home
And when I begin to break down,
In you I will do the same

You always have my hand, my love
In warmth and tenderly
To wipe the tears from your eyes
That in strength will not betray
That in trust will hold you gently
In a promise and a kiss

That I won't go away
That from you, won't wonder off or go astray

As I hope unto your broken heart
That that's not too much to say
And that in the glow of two as one with me
You'll want to stay

Creation Set Free

She's gone to a secret place
To a place where the sun sets west
To a place where there is an open door
A place that must be addressed
With the heart of a child
And a spirit set free

To love this world from futility
All green, set loose
Left without restraint
That over flows in its fullness
Of a heavenly garden set loose
That unfolds unto earth

She stands in the center
As it overflows
Overwhelming, as in spirit it grows

She is the key to the door
That holds it back
As in one with her
We turn the handle
To see it all burst forth
Beyond the boundaries
Of its former prison

To find, out of control
In wild disbandment
All of creation reborn
As a child alive has risen

This is but one cry of my lover's heart
As in one we create this brand new state
As it comes forth in our midst
To manifest

As a new world comes to birth
A new heaven and a new earth
Now ascends and meets
Its hunger's cry

In the Glance of a Hurricane

I've seen a lot of places rage;
I've seen a lot of places rock and roll,
But I've never seen a place like this explode.

It was an inferno
In a glance of a girl on fire in dance.
Three hundred dancing in one romance,
A place of fallen walls
Of unbridled passion unrehearsed.
To the silence of the setting sun
To the avalanche of the moon's glow
Come undone

Captured in another time
In the spirit of another place,
Swirling in a hurricane,
All masks taken away from our face.
In an almost oneness,
Something divine in play.

That loses the air, to breath in deep.
If just for a moment,
In wild enchantment
Freed from our clay.

You can feel the static electricity
Pulsing threw life's veins.
You can smell the freshness of the air
Of a spring shower that washes away times stain
Layers peel in anticipation
As songs' lightning strike the heart
That in an instant strips away
Self-condemnation that blows tame denial apart.

In a Ray of Hope

Leering from behind her eyes
A ray of hope lays in wait in surprise
A mystery kept right beneath the skin

Patient for a time to escape, to be revealed
At the right moment not to hesitate,
To unleash in one cloud's burst
To in a field of fire, quench a world of thirst

To see a profusion of living colors
In a garden that overflows
Beyond the fringe of what can be imagined
Where all that can be heard
Becomes yes, instead of no

A seed that explodes into a million more
Everyone a freedom spore
As to the ground each drop of water falls
In a dream fulfilled

As the rain it pours, each drop a rainbow promise
That as it hits begins to unfold,
As the drop of tears my lover cries in joy,
Is another world come to birth
That grows forever nearer.

Love Restored

Tonight I burst out of my prison
Into the liberation of my lovers arms
Disarmed as she comes for me from above
As she unfolds her wings
With her cloak, blowing in the wind
All bright, a mile behind her.

In the cold of the darkest night
Torn out of my place
Into a different space
Rising out of the ashes
That once was me
Into another world
That now I come to see
A place alive, set free

That swallows me
Held in her love
In a realm of no futility

Where I hold her in the green
In the mist of Heaven

Looking up at His morning stars
Shimmering in His glory
Nothing held in reserve
Just to come into His promises kept
In the restoration of His love
In her and in me
We are set free

Captured in Your Green Array

The beautiful gems in your head
The bars of light from your prisms
Shed in green array of emerald blades
That cut straight through me
Through the stone and rock around my heart,
The armor that no one could break through.

In one single glance, I did not stand a chance
Like a pin put to a balloon it blew,
Apart in all directions all the pieces flew.
To leave me open wide and vulnerable
To the touch of you

In the hand that she took that led me away
That loosed me from the prison in which I dwelled
To see the chains fall from me
And from my eternal night
Bear witness to the dawning day

Unbeknownst and Unseen Woman of My Dreams

Unbeknownst to the world around
Walking in the rhythm of the night
In the midst of the shadows
Her name known only to the sound of silence
That whispers in her ear

The wind, the word spoken
Draped in the unknown of the dark
Residing sharply on the edge of a razor
Sheer and stark she cuts the air
Her form sleekly passing through the rifts and tears
That glides between two separate worlds

Bridged in the motion where her feet brush the ground
Almost afloat her silhouette
Almost as heavy as she
That fills the gap in the frame of two doors

Unhinged, wide open
Where her sun and moon in her mid-heaven collide

That in the grace of the light that surrounds her
Still to wake within her where a thousand dreams abide

To My Fairy Queen

I see a star spilling flame
That rains in sheets of gold,
Within the night
Consumed in blue light
As two birds in flight take hold.

The wind raps round us like a cloak,
That sings the song of the wild,
That whispers words never heard
Known only to the hearts of a child.

We dance on air my lady fair,
Within our majestic stare.
In hands so warm,
Of fires adorned,
That spark your eyes of joy.

The angels play
In white array

A melody just for you.
As we melt into an avalanche
We make one drop of water
Where once there was two

She Has the Prettiest Face

She has the prettiest face in the world,
Indefinable by human words
That if could be spoken
Would crack the glass between heaven and earth
And fracture the columns in between the two worlds.

The one that I'm in love with
Amongst a thousand faces
Hers is the only one that I see
When I wake up and when I go to sleep
She is the one of my dreams

Whether my eyes are wide open
Or whether they are closed
She's the one who can see that deeply inside of me

The only one to whom my depths I have shown
To be able to see the forest through the trees
Who doesn't leave me feeling all alone.

A Place Where Our Eyes Collide

She has the loveliest eyes I've seen
Between Heaven and Earth they beam
Like stars from the Heavens they peer into me
In warmth from her soothing greens
That shine a light in my depths a place that few have seen
Only the smile of an angel with green eyes can hold me in my dreams
Pale skin so white her arms so tight that cradle the likes of me

My china doll of ivory, that in jest has set me free
A place on high beyond men's hands
Beyond their hating hearts
A place of tears made from joy
A place that knows no fear

Where hope becomes a song so sweet
Beneath a rainbow seat
A promise kept in the night
A love that's made complete

Cupped in the hands of the Father
As from it he takes a drink
Of the taste alive of living water
As this heaviness starts to sink
Away from clay of two now one
Embraced forever in His home
In one reside his daughter and son.

In One Love of One Song

From the top of the mountain
To the valley down below
To the crest of life to where the water flows
Taken in form to life on earth
In the shape of a girl spilling of fire
Her hands so warm
She takes the lightening from the storm
As her thunder overflows
That fills the skies with her light
In love that is adorned.

To the dance of the ocean's curve
To the harp of an angel's voice
She dances like a skater's pirouette
Her face the moon reflects her soul
The fires of a volcano erupt
Held in her control

Conformed not confined
To the rising of a brand new day

Of this light of dawn splitting the sky
Of a time that's been waiting forever long that has come,
Our hands together in harmony
In one love of one song.

Where My Lover Waits

In enchanted lands
Where I meet you
In a state of dream

In the hidden forest primeval
Unseen, beneath a sky in the night
Full of fireflies
Each one a fairy in disguise, swarming

In song, in joy, divine
In dance, two children frolic
Through the trees
Under a shower of blue and silver
Snowflakes of light fluttering all around

As the brilliant shadows hit the ground
You take my hand dripping with mischief
Your face all aglow
That melts all the way through the snow.

As our heat together flows into one light
Peering into a snow globe of the world
To feel its afterglow to its setting

In the crack between Earth and Heaven
We gradually awake to the birth of a new day
As we rise, our eyes are greeted by the sun's rays

Though still covered in the gentle chill of sleep
As it slowly fades, I lovingly awake
In foreknowing the forthcoming of my loves gate.

The Lights Behind the Scene

There are many lights on Broadway
But none has ever shown brighter than you
Not every light is on the stage
There are lights behind the scenes too

That makes it possible
For them to shine so bright
But who really knows this, very few

Voices that are not vocal, sometime speak the loudest
They are not heard through the spoken word
But resonate through the house
That pronounced reverberates
In its projection from their mouths

In front, the audience
Rising to their feet in applause
As it pours out

But when the curtain falls
And the applause dies down
And the cast takes a curtain call
And bows

When all is said and done
And the actors have all left
And the crowds get out of town
And all is silent, not even a cricket to be found

You are the one that is still around
And though the sense of loneliness fills the air
The apron in place
The energy of the night resides
That fills you full of wonder
That in your excitement sounds like thunder
As inside the child of mystery abounds

Time

As the last grain of sand falls
Through the hips of the hour glass,
Spinning slowly into oblivion
And the sea of time stills
I want to gaze into your eyes and see
The reflection in your smile,
Of time setting, setting beneath the horizon.

As the last second unwinds, to be never found again.
As our perception changes, from a shadow into light;
Holding your hands
Only the new shared with you
Coming into sight

A Moment Tender Caught in Time

(Part I)

As I trace the railroad tracks of your ear,
To the point where your neck meets your head.
You whisper something to me.

All of my fingers follow the lines of your jaw
That crosses over your lips.

A tear of love rolls down my face from what you said
That echoes in the caverns of my soul eternal.

A Moment Tender Captured in Dream

(Part II)

She sits in my lap, almost asleep
Speaking in tongues, unaware of what it was
All I know is that it was deep

My arms around her, warm and soft
Her head cradled on my shoulder
Both together, high up in a loft
In a place not here on earth

In the hold of a dream's live wire
In one vision, whimsical of a hidden touch
Out of reach, out of view
Of a world with brutal hands
Held within an embrace

In a kiss gentle held sacred in trust that's true
Nestled secure, held insured
In a fortress with no walls, no doors, no floors

Just a light from above,
As the stars watch over us

Shrouded in silence, raining in solace
As each snowflake in white blue
Cascades into a blanket of warmth inside the cold
In the touch of a gentle love so true

My Vision of Vienna

My love I want to go with you to Vienna
To hear a symphony of lights displayed
That falls in sparks of fireworks
Above our heads

Bursting, dancing, swirling to the song of life
In our hearts unfolding all around
Becoming alive in the midst of our footsteps being revealed
In revelation to the sound of the laughter of what is young
That we feel in us conveyed.

Of two free spirits
Sharing one voice
Of a child set free in love

In the Heart of Vienna

In the reverence of a golden night
Consumed in the lights of Vienna
Our hands clenched in the pocket of warmth
Our fingers locked in a glow adorned

Walking through a symposium
An orchestra roaring all around
In sight and in sound
Swirling, taken to flight

A sonnet captured in revelry
That takes form put to song
That abounds, as our feet
Move in time to the rush of the waves that cascade upon us

Of the air crackling, with electricity
That in our gaze of a smile set ablaze
Electric in a touch

That astounds in the taste of sweet
Of candy lips that of a moment captured in time, drips

Drenched in life set free
A photograph of the soul captured forever in a glance
In the eyes of an epic that unfolds
Playing out in the harmony of a lovers dance

The Glow of the Magic Beans

The blackest coffee in the world,
The strongest thickest brew,
Not known to many on the earth
Drank only by a few.

This potion of danger, comes in one form
Almost deadly to the taste.
That makes your nerves stand up on end
That makes you want to double in half
That makes your eyes want to burst.

That will cause the strongest legs to bend,
And die of a lack of thirst.
A challenge to many pro-extremists
With stomachs cast in steel,
But only a few adventurers have managed to survive the ordeal.

Legend has it comes from some strange mountain peak.

Grown in the heart of the jungle
Danced to by Amazon feet.

The beans are said to glow beneath
A silver full moon,
Mesmerizing all who gaze upon
The magic beans of doom.

Tiramisu

My lovely little tiramisu
Creamy and sweet
Deliciously decadent and deadly are you.

Just thinking of you could make me fat,
I'll be your bad baby and you'll be mine
My sweet dessert that is divine.

So dance with me beneath the silvery moon
My little sweetie to the rapture of calypso tunes
In the midst of the unfolding night.

And squeeze me tight
To the song of the ocean
Upon her golden dunes

My Little Lass

My little lass dance with me a jig
To the heat of an open furnace burning
The auburn glow upon your face on fire
Overflowing in a smile alive

The molten lava from your raging heart flowing
The scent of rosewood mixed with sweat
As it drips upon the floor
Each pearl a drop of life in motion
As together our spirits soar.

To see you unleashed and your wild untamed set free
As you let loose a blood curdling scream
I feel the burn of the infernos in your eyes escape into mine
Our hearts pounding to the drums I feel in you
Oceans colliding, our hands together to the rhythm of a raging sea
Crashing on a shore of gold

Its shimmering light, our one delight
As the magic of this night takes hold

A Knock at the Door

She's pretty and sharp and playful and sweet
My closet lover, dangerously discreet
A knock at the door
A whisper on the floor
As she stamps on by
On the wings of an eagle

As she looks into me
With a mischievous smile, so severe
Then just sings,
Touching me invisibly
Cutting deep with those eyes

My slice of heaven, wrapped tight
In skin, my purring kitten
With mysterious green eyes

And I am her puppy dog
With sad skies

That clear up to the sound of her pounding heart

That dry up the rain
And make it shine in this lonely heart
No more of mine, given to her
Held in her hand
As in the storm of her love
With her I stand.

Sacred, Secret, Sweetie

She runs down my mouth
Like biting into a ripe peach
Like cream, my secret lover
Sweet and discreet

The scent of a wind, blown
Filled with lilac
Incognito, she moves swiftly through my nights
Greeting my mornings
Whispering softly with a smile
Impish in my eye of what she has to say

Then vanishes with one glance
Austere, the sound of trickling water
On a Midsummer's Day
A cool brook flowing tells me
She's not far away

The taste in the air of vanilla

An extract, the mellow spice of life
With just a hint of cinnamon, robust
That burns away the strife
That which is hidden
Puts a hint of something grand in life
Sparkling in your eye

The touch of velvet near your skin
As her shadow in me digs in
Approaching me from all directions
As finally the sun sets on this day

As now we continue to play
Now that the cat has gone away
And there's no one around to say
Mans' favorite word, NO!

We shed these chains.
We move in time
In the rhythm of the blue moon
As its light rains upon us

To the ambrosia of the whaling of a saxophone
Unleashed, untamed, set out on its own
To rage
In an embrace of our unknown

One, Hot, Kiss

She takes me down like a wildebeest
In the Serengeti
A lioness in control

Her claws dig in her teeth rip and tear
As she drinks the blood of my soul

Like a glass of wine
As a Chabot, as her cup overflows
Drowning in the essence of my being
Until we feel like we both might explode
Enthralled in celebration, set loose at a fiesta

Our hearts pounding to almost burst
Jubilant to the taste of life, set free in a kiss,
The juices of her loins flowing
The scent of the wild in disbandment
No longer under control

Exposed to what truly is no longer held in reserve
As she licks me off her lips
And I spill down her throat
Like an elixir in love

Warm into her belly
Soft, a violent touch, shared in the spark
Of two laying as one
In the embrace of the tender upon her face

That to the touch, that's cream like lace
As her lines with my fingers I trace
So silent her sigh
Her breath I take engaged our lips together
So soft to the touch that's shared between us
One overwhelmed in the light of grace

Climax!

Making love in the blanket of a spring rain
The sky all blue
The drops pelt off the window pane

Streaming down the sill
In an orchestra's array
To the rhythm of an ocean in motion
As it plays calypso.

To the thumping of a June's pale blue moon
Symbiotic, two entities that now make a whole
That embrace each other's loneliness
No longer left in the cold

That no longer, now that together
Left without, as completed
Joined they take hold

We steam up the windows

With our heat
As each bead of sweat, collects, drips
That boils into air
As it sprays across the room

The pressure building
The sound shrilling
The electric spilling into lightening chilling
As all around it begins to break
The wind reeling, a cyclone we are feeling
As we escalate, swelling to Toccata and D Fuge in Minor

As we annihilate the calm
Of a fragile world at peace
As we reach a final state
Of destination within our relations
Of a now very hot cold war

All the sirens sound the raging sea
Astounding as from the heavens the fire begins
To pour as to the sound of a final gasp
Where it harkens, the spirits rein.

Hot!

To taste the wine of your breath
That spills off of your lips into my mouth.
A kiss of your essence divine,
So sweet the taste of your heart pounding next to mine.
That ripples through my skin electric
As the fires glow into as one shines

I feel the blood course through our veins,
Pulsing to almost burst.
Enwrapped in rapture, in one thrust
As together we quench our thirst

The sweat, it ruptures from our skin
As we meld, held so close
That boils, that steams, into fog
As your metal forged in me smelts.

Into her eyes of a green infernos,
I fall into her soul,

Her toning, moaning--our choir in time
As she takes over me in control.

Her scent alluring as I taste her pheromones;
Hypnotized in the glow of a detonations aftermath.
As in release, I see her afterglow,
The sun setting on the wake of a massive earthquake
Falling into a full moon,
Rising as it disappears beneath the horizon
Into a state of dreams

The Burning Thread of Your Whisper

Her voice as sharp as a razor,
The song she sings rips out my heart.
The briars and barbs stick in me,
As I drink the thorny blood of her soul.

As on fire, she screams,
Answering my darkest desire
With sweetness that causes my wounds to burn.

No soothing for my spearing heart
Baking in my own juices, I squirm
My being in her love blown apart.

Her eyes open doorways,
In an angel's sigh of joy,
Her distance closes
Only the wings creating a breeze.
Falling into the bursting sun

Entering her realm of dreams.

We meet, our lips engage,
Our mouths lock
Feeling the chill of our touching noses,
Fascinated at the mystery
My melting lover imposes.

My Taste of Delight

My love discreet, my closet diva
Use me and make my lap your seat
I want you to be the woman in my dreams
I want you to be my lover supreme

I want to taste all thirty-one flavors of you in delight
I want you to take me to flight into the majesty of your heart
Beneath the shimmering moonlight all blue
Over New York City tonight

I want to melt into the great unknown in you
In a place out of sight
To taste your lips in another world
And behold in all of your might

My Little Liquid Electric Love

My little liquid electric love
You get under my skin
And make my blood boil.

When I see you dance
In a blanket of romance
The potion pounding through me,
Takes the breath from within my heart
Aroused now in a state of ambiance.

Burning in your fire
As the crystal bells sound,
In the drum beat of desire
That rings of the song you sing
From the depths of an angel's fire.

The light you shine abounds, overwhelms and astounds
In the blast of trumpets golden array to your motion
I hear a thunderous orchestra play

As I watch you dip and sway.

A thousand worlds open wide;
A field of orchids from up on high
Unfold before my eyes.
Captured in the wake of a moment
As it comes to birth.
Amazed in a glance, you caught my eye
And reached out to me your hand,
As I rise to my feet all a quiver, within you I stand.

Salt

She smells like New York City
She tastes like the Atlantic
All salty, the spice of life

She looks like the sun setting over Hawaii
Her lines as sharp as a knife
The smack of a kiss of her hand upon my face
As she holds my head in her embrace of lace

Then draws it near to her heart
As to me her love she imparts
Her tough love, the kindest I've ever felt
As in the lights of a oneness with her, I melt

When Ships Collide

It was in a jazzy, bluesy, smoke-filled bar
A cocktail in my hand
It was just around the midnight hour
When I saw that she walked in

Rapped all around within a long coat
Covered up very well
But you knew that beneath the overcoat
She was dressed for sin

Her eyes met mine
And drove us to each other
I asked her if she would like a drink
And if there was a worry
That needed to be smothered
She told me her name

I felt it just the same
That lit up the air, like magic

As it spilled from the ruby lips of this dame

As the essence of her ambiance
Permeated the room
Like cheap perfume
That in a daze, tantalized me
Arousing the empty space inside

Every word, new
Exactly the places I hide
So no one can see the Swiss cheese in me
Though, as hard as I tried
I couldn't escape
That which I could not deny

That in her secret feminine ways
That which within she had entered inside
Was by this damsel in distress
She set my heart ablaze

There was the possibility that
Two ships did collide

Two Unlikely Champions

You are Red Rider and I am Seabiscuit
Two unlikely champions
That collided, brought together
By the hands of faith.

For you, my love, I'd wait for eternity to come and go
For the end of time as its hands begin to slow
Until stars fall out of view
I'd wait forever to dance with you

To burn in your arms eternal
Set ablaze by your eyes that touch me like green fusion
That when meet and mingle with my baby blues
Sees past all of life's illusion
That breaks apart in the gaze
Of a thousand church bells ringing

To a choir of a thousand angels
As we kiss and swirl in a hurricane unto the song

Of that which their singing,
That rains upon us
In heavenly lights
As all other lights begin to fade
And everything else in sight starts to wane

Check Point Charlie

Call it Check Point Charlie
The concentration camp of the mind
Of capitulation
Of being conditioned by legal slime

When from behind me I heard a thought from a heart divine
Saying to me, "turn around."
There she stood as she whispered in my ear
Let's get out of this place.

We slowly walked out leaving the door behind
As she took my hand and we declined
The poison they offered
And walked toward what in periwinkle shined

We look at each other
Giddy, and smiled
As we entered gold defined
And to God's kingdom

Taken into open arms in an embrace
That won't betray

Waiting for us to come
At the point of our arrival
As we now leave the hatred of a world of clay

A Trip to Starbucks

Coffee lady,
Voice of a thousand harps,
Harmoniously entering my mind.
Scrambling my thoughts.

Melting the layers of tar and nicotine,
Tying up my tongue
So that I can't speak.
Making my mind like jelly,

Quivering, my knees barely standing.
My pulse pounding weak.
Your words like clouds impale me
Boiling my blood,
Bursting my organs,
Ripping out my guts.

Your soft-spoken walk,
Your body talk,

A smile that defiles my stony heart;
That lines my body's shadow
On the floor in chalk.

With kindness so warm
That it is poison to the human hardness of this life.
That cuts deep into the protection of lonely strife.

That tears the door of gloom off its hinge,
That with sweetness in my soul is a knife,
Killing my closed mind of thoughts
That there is no one like you left.

The Platinum Girl from NYC

The platinum girl from NYC
The bad ass chic from the Moulin Rouge
The only one that could make me amused
That makes me feel so free

Combat boots, my soldier true
Her heart so broken it made me blue
Of bittersweet that melts in me
Through her eyes of green

Her voice like an angel that comforts me
To hear her sing, to feel her heat
Spill into me from her willow tree
That made me believe.

She dances like David before the Lord
Her love I can't ignore
That takes me by my head and hand
That makes my spirit soar.

Into the blue of the night
Glazed like icing on a cake
Running down the Boulevard
Spinning round the street lights
As on fire in wild in love we make
The darkness glow of amber ways

That spills on earth alive from heavenly pearls
That hit the ground as in youth together we strive.
Where your wild abandon and my being thrive.

My Lovely Little Villain

There she was smoking a cigar
My little Bonnie decked out like calamity Jane
Her six shooters by her side
Looking as though she is about to ride
Into the setting of the sun

Two gangsters in heat
In love on the run
Notorious, our names well known
That dread unto faces of everyone
I ride with her with golden spurs
Made from the treasure we've won

To the rest of the world, a danger unsung
To me, my kitten that in my arms purrs to the fallen sun.

My Little Gypsy Queen

My little lass, my gypsy queen
Rage with me around the fire tonight
Pull me up from my cup of grog
And yank me to your chest

Through the sparks and smoke, as we collide
To the fiddle, where in one embrace we abide
Captured in the cantor to the song
Of a storm on the horizon, bursting,
Unleashed to the sound of a coyote
In the distance crying

Unto the call of the wild
From the violent joy that escapes
From deep inside of you
That quivers through the marrow in my bones
That churns the blood in my veins
That ripples through me like the wind
That quakes my soul

To the quickness that brings my heart to life

A shrill that makes the Heavens spill
That tears the very air,
That makes the bright, brighter still
As my well, your rain it fills

A Place Within

She unties the knots in me
Each one a fear and tear in my field of wheat
That grows inside of me
That shines beneath the golden sun
That ripples like waves on fire
As through me, the wind blows

She holds me in her hand of living water
Now made clean and clear as she drinks me in
To her heart made brand new
In the mouth of God's daughter

Enraptured in her embrace
In Heaven's blue
In a kiss of her sweet
She calls me Starling
I call her my turtle dove

Flying in the midst of a crystal city made of light

As the light shines in our eyes from above
In a place where we touch unseen
Not known to man's sight
I hold her in mid-flight as her hands I clench

The Other Side of the Mirror

My lover on the other side of the mirror
The reflection I see staring back at me
In a place between just one face

The flip side of a reality, consciously unconscious
The sublime hidden between the eyes so thin and so sleek
Almost invisible the split of dangers that separates between
The cracks of time

Caught in place of motionlessness
That in this mirror
In your reflection caught in my eye
Your part of me revealed
As I put my hands to yours, the slice of just one

My Spiritual Dream

My lover my queen
My spiritual dream
Into your arms I come

To fill the gap between the light
To feel the warmth of the sun
That shines upon your face like the moon
That is an open door

That invites me into your deepest room
To the center of your core
A world of prefusion
Of creation about ready to take form

To be a spark, felt in the dark
As upon your desert bursts forth a storm.
Where the horses run wild
In the heart of a child
Hidden behind a woman's mind.

The two of you, wrapped into one
A mystery left undefined
In the blood of the heat of a gypsy dancer

As To Her Dreams I Sway

I am the immovable object
And you are the unstoppable force
And when we make love and collide
The earth trembles, the pillars shake to almost crumble

As that which is between Heaven and Earth breaks,
The sky it falls to the ground as it rips open and bleeds fire and ruptures
As it detonates in your desert heart
The force of thunder's choir
The lightening turns the sand into glass

That bursts and shatters
Set free from its coat of molten clay, now blown away
Your calm now left in the past
I cannot deny you.

I cannot walk away from you
From your wanting eyes of longing green

From you I cannot stray
Your embrace of steel holds me for real
That I cannot escape, beneath your love's enthralling wait.

All the layers of epidermis peals
As light as a feather with the force of a freight train
I do not want to leave from here
The touch of an angel
Her halo slightly stained
Covered in a blanket of what is warm
Her bare body upon me
Like the coolest summer rain.

That relieves my thirst
In a dance unrehearsed
And removes every ounce of pain.
As to her dreams I sway.

My Heart

Though it may be gusty and snowy outside
That chills you to the bone
Before you resides
A cottage that's cozy and warm inside

That is my heart that receives you as a home
The door is always open
Just come on in

The fire is always stoked and glowing
And its warmth is always flowing
Worn-in couches and comforters
Wait for your arrival

To hold you inside this glowing embrace
To melt the cold away from your face
To see it shine in the auburn lights
From my fireplace.

Where My Lover Waits

In enchanted lands
Where I meet you
In a state of dreams

In the hidden forest primeval
Unseen, beneath a sky in the night
Full of fireflies
Each one a fairy in disguise, swarming

In song, in joy, divine
In dance, two children frolic
Through the trees
Under a shower of blue and silver
Snowflakes of light, fluttering all around

As the brilliant shadows hit the ground,
You take my hand, dripping with mischief,
Your face all aglow
That melts all the way through the snow.

As our heat together flows into one light
Peering into a snow globe of the world
To feel its afterglow to its setting

In the crack between earth and heaven,
We gradually awake to the birth of a new day
As we rise, our eyes are greeted by the sun's rays

Though still covered in the gentle chill of sleep
As it slowly fades, I lovingly awake
In foreknowing the forthcoming of my love's gate.

A Place Where Our Eyes Collide

She has the most lovely eyes I've seen
Between heaven and earth they beam
Like stars from the heavens, they peer into me
In warmth from her soothing greens
That shine a light in my depths, a place that few have seen
Only the smile of an angel with green eyes can hold me in my dreams
Pale skin so white her arms so tight that cradle the likes of me

My china doll of ivory that in jest has set me free
A place on high beyond men's hands
Beyond their hating hearts
A place of tears made from joy
A place that knows no fear

Where hope becomes a song so sweet
Beneath a rainbow seat
A promise kept in the night
A love that's made complete

Cupped in the hands of the Father
As from it, He takes a drink
Of the taste alive of living water
As this heaviness starts to sink
Away from clay of two now one
Embraced forever in His home
In one reside His daughter and son.

In the Eyes of a Stranger

In the smoky bar, she sits not so far away
Her eyes following me
As I stamp out my butt in the ashtray
The jazz roaring as the trumpet plays
As incognito her energy dips and sways
To the motion of the ocean
From the music's waves
That careens upon our shores

Soaking in intrigue its effervescent sprays
She just winks, then looks away
Her pounding heart speaks to me
Without a word to say
The saxophone wails
Steeped in New York City blues

I stare out the window as from night
The 12 o'clock hour ensues
To feel the pounding life of the city

That will never sleep
Turn in the hands of time
Set on edge, drenched in two different dreamers
Lonely hearted blues

She walks over to me, her hips, they sway
And asks me if the seat is taken
She takes the seat and shuffles her feet
To the beat of the song the band is playing
As to the ambrosia of the rhythm
Her head and neck swaying
Knowing it's nice to be lonely with someone

As two strangers become familiar
Over a glass of spirits, she reaches out,
And takes my hand
And leads me to the dance floor
That breaks the chill of all my ills
As her sultry lines merge with me
In the offering of a glance
Soaked warm in romance
As the embers glow
Brightened in the kiss of a dance

In This Dream That's Real

My ghostly, deadly shadow dancing
A silhouette so sharp that cuts through my skin
Like a knife through butter
Her smile of mischief so bright
It burns right thru to the other side of my life force

As to my depths she exposes daylight to my night
Effervescent, clear, almost invisible
In tangent her touch that I feel so much
Impales me enraptured in her fingertips

Her breath filling me
As now we become indivisible
In the light that's shared in between entangled together
That has set us free

From boundaries imposed, and the walls that enclose
Us held within this mortal coil
Now shed as we take off our clothes

That is this limitation that now removed
We can expose what's beneath the skin

So held within this grasp of life
Has now released that once was
A caterpillar escapes into its cocoon
To find in rebirth life made brand new.

As a butterfly unfolds its wings to the sound of what freedom sings
And the colors to a world anew brings life
Unleashed into a kingdom that awaits our coming
Into a place without any boundaries

Our past left behind as we enter into a world that's defined
In transparent gold, in streets purely refined
This I see my one so near
Behind your eyes that show no fear
That comes into me, made so clear

In the crystal city in joy shed as a tear

The Knights of the Light

Before a world of broken dreams
Beneath a heavy sky
We stand as one
As the lies come undone
In a future filled with hope!

In whatever rubble filled the halls,
Whatever must be done
We stand in the presence of the Lord
To become His freedom daughters and sons

One Nation, under God
With wings of eagles that do not stop,
That fills the Will of Jehovah
In the promise of His word that will never drop.

Our heroes fight in righteousness
To change this world of hate
Taking the hand of destiny

And removing the chance in fate.

The women and men of God's Country they defend
To become his Knights of honor
To cut the heal of the Living Dead
To in light fill the darkness with dread
To see the darkness scatter seven ways
Before the Light of the Lord.

To see our Nation in revelation
To be given to one accord
To see the flag of this country fly
In God's Knights' grace
To see the Glory He imparts
Shine upon our face.

To be the Sons of Liberty
That makes us what we are
To see the rising over this world
Of the morning star.

Wherever You Stand

A princess adorned
In gems all aglow
Each one a revelation
Of God's will upon the cusp to come.

You are my beautiful one
Full of the light of the Son
Of golden burning bright
Blinding in the eyes of my spirit's sight.

That makes the air crackle
Wherever you stand
That takes the land in His name
Wherever you place your feet
To see His glory overflow at the wake of His enemy's defeat.

I've Seen the Spirit Cry

I've seen your spirit cry fifty thousand tears
All violet and silver
Each drop that falls upon the earth
Is a need met.

In the midst of a human life, set free,
That touches the hearts of mortal men,
That melts away this strife.

That can change tears of sorrow
Into tears of joy.
That brings forth a hope
For a new tomorrow,
Invested in love that is divine
As we drink the living wine.

That flows from the seed held deep inside
That cries for its release to over exceed our borders
To leave our boundaries behind.

You are my love an arrow true,
Shot from cupid into my heart
The only one to get through
My armor blown apart.

Left exposed to the touch of a glance
That is almost too much
Held within your gentle hands
My life unto you I trust

Beyond the hate that man can do
Beyond the lying tongue
Your words to me, I've never heard
Beyond lips to me that are sung.

I see upon your face a sea
A never ending road,
A journey to a great unknown
As a star inside you explodes.

Alive in birth to be the first
Of many to come forth
To have the word burned into your heart
That which is refined as sacred
That which is refined as sacred that is set apart.

To reign forth in you
To become something new never seen before

To take the step
Our hands entangled
That no one else wants to

For all its worth to give up all and open up the door
To stand with me into the face of truth
To stand with us as one
To let His love overwhelm our own
And unto Him become.

When All Seemed Lost

My head in my hands
Tears begin to swim as they spill from the pools forming in my eyes
Bursting on the ground
In the darkened room in which I sit
Alone, hoping in the quiet thunder in my soul
Breaking, that you will return

Standing in front of this empty room
Where the still air around me feels like the chill of a tomb
I pick up a drink to numb of what I think
To know you're not around
And drop it to the floor
As in front of me I find you there

Open wide your arms and me collide
Embrace in a light that cannot hide
This feeling that fills this empty dark room
That in me subsides in the wake of a dawning day

Not covered in grey

With no longer walls to divide, only the pallets gleam
The brilliance of two melting in a place up on high

Walking in Heaven

Walking down the boardwalk at 2 a.m.
Seeing and feeling the profusion of colors culminate into one
As the spirit touches the earth the sky opens wide
Nothing in the way

Her hand in my back pocket
Mine in hers
Everyone else so far away

Together walking, no one else around
Just the sound of the footsteps talking
The voice of the ocean
As it crashes its heart pounding so violently loud

The winter sigh, the wind of a shattered flute
That calls our names together in her touch
That feels so warm, held in her arms

In the heart of heaven

Where in God's arms we are clutched
In through her portholes
I see a thousand of these

It's like each and every one
Is a bubble filled with liquid rainbow
Each one a different world
Of scent, of flavor, and of colors

All a promise kept as it all becomes real
Unseen to the world outside
As deeper into the center
The layers begin to peel
A field of dreams that unfolds like wings of a butterfly
As in my sight are revealed

God's Word to You

The eyes in your head
A light I've never seen.
That glow green from above
That in me beam.

The glow around you shines
Gold from heaven above,
That melts into me
In your grip of love.

You have no clue, just what you are
A beacon in the night
That holds me close like no other has ever done.

That fills me up
That holds me tight
That never lets me go.

That cannot linger, that in my midst

Is as pure as a dove.
I call your name
It sounds like an angel crying
That fills the space between Heaven and Earth.

In tears of joy from above
You take my hand
From the world that to me is sand
And cups me in your heart
That feels like cold water
In the heat of the sun.

Where the Sun Split the Heavens

Every time I see the sun come into view
That breaks the line of the horizon of the sky
I feel brand new, I cry with you
To vent it out for the very last time
And break the chains of our yokes
And leave it all behind

To shed a tear for the past
Of this poison rain
To find the doors left open in waiting
To strangle all our genes
And to see those eyes restored again
Everything made clear, we dance

In the midst of the clouds
In the heavens as we push the ladder down
Out of reach from the hands of the hating hearts
And the mouths of the Baskervilles Hellhounds

I take your hands
You take my heart
Held gentle that astounds
And pull me here into you bosom
And in a love we drown

Surrounded in the light
We hold on tight
To feel a smile revealed
To the joy of being one in spirit inside

Healed as the orange is pealed
To live behind the stain inside
And as the wonder of us is revealed
To become the expression in God Divine
And to know that it is sealed.

CPSIA information can be obtained at www.ICGtesting.com
Printed in the USA
BVOW070424200112

280918BV00001B/33/P